THE PANAMA CANAL

BY PETER BENOIT

CHILDREN'S PRESS®

An Imprint of Scholastic Inc.

New York   Toronto   London   Auckland   Sydney

Mexico City   New Delhi   Hong Kong

Danbury, Connecticut

BRINGING HISTORY to LIFE

Content Consultant
James Marten, PhD
Professor and Chair, History Department
Marquette University
Milwaukee, Wisconsin

Library of Congress Cataloging-in-Publication Data
Benoit, Peter, 1955–
    The Panama Canal / by Peter Benoit.
        pages cm.—(Cornerstones of freedom.)
    Includes bibliographical references and index.
    ISBN 978-0-531-28205-2 (lib. bdg.) — ISBN 978-0-531-27670-9 (pbk.)
    . Panama Canal (Panama)—History—Juvenile literature. 2. Canals—
    Panama—Design and construction—History—Juvenile literature. 3.
    Canal Zone—History—Juvenile literature. I. Title.
    F1569.C2B47 2014
    972.87'5—dc23   2013002373

    2 3 4 5 6 7 8 9 10 R 23 22 21 20 19 18 17 16 15 14

Photographs © 2014: AP Images: 40 (North Wind Picture Archives), 6
(Panama Canal Commission); Art Resource/The New York Public Library:
1, 13; Charlene W. Padgett: 47 (In honor of William Eugene Ferrar
Padgett, Sr.); Corbis Images: back cover (Frans Lanting), 49 (Underwood
& Underwood), 16; Dreamstime: 55 (Gira), 54 (Picturemakersllc); Getty
Images: cover (Hulton Archive), 39 (Time Life Pictures/Panama Canal Photo);
Library of Congress: 2, 3, 7, 12, 21, 22, 24, 26, 33, 36, 44, 46, 48, 56 bottom, 57;
Smithsonian Institution Libraries, Washington, D.C.: 32; Superstock, Inc.: 5
top, 10, Inc.: 15 (DeAgostini), 4 bottom, 14, 30 (Everett Collection), 34, 35, 41
Everett Collection), 8 (H-D Falkenstein/ima / imagebroker.net), 20, 56 top
Jaime Abecasis/imageb/imagebroker.net), 42 (Thompson Paul/Prisma); The
Granger Collection: 5 bottom, 28; The Image Works: 4 top, 17, (Mary Evans
Picture Library), 43 (Mary Evans/Pharcide), 19 (NMPFT/SSPL), 37, 38, 29 (SZ
Photo/Scherl); XNR Productions, Inc.: 52, 53.

Did you know that studying history can be fun?

BRING HISTORY TO LIFE by becoming a history investigator. Examine the evidence (primary and secondary source materials); cross-examine the people and witnesses. Take a look at what was happening at the time—but be careful! What happened years ago might suddenly become incredibly interesting and change the way you think!

Contents

Searching for a Shortcut

In 1513, Vasco Núñez de Balboa led the first European expedition across the Americas to the Pacific Ocean.

The dream of digging a canal to connect the Atlantic and Pacific Oceans was born 500 years ago. In 1513, Spanish explorer Vasco Núñez de Balboa set out from what is now Panama to find a water route between the two oceans. He was surprised to find that they were separated by only a narrow strip of mountains and jungles. King Charles I of Spain ordered a survey of the land. It was soon determined that building a canal through Panama would be impossible. The dream was set aside for more than 300 years. During that time, the world changed greatly. One of the biggest changes was the formation of the United States of America on the East Coast of North America in 1776.

The discovery of gold in 1848 at Sutter's Mill in California encouraged thousands of Americans to travel westward in search of fortune. This created renewed interest in a canal that could shorten the time needed to move passengers westward and gold back east. Traveling from one coast to the other required a long and dangerous trip, whether by land or by sea.

Sawmill operator James Marshall (below) discovered gold in California in 1848, kicking off a gold rush that lasted several years.

MINED DURING THE CALIFORNIA GOLD RUSH

CHAPTER 1

A ROCKY START

Before the construction of the Panama Canal, the only way to travel by boat between the Atlantic and Pacific Oceans was to sail all the way around South America.

A CANAL THROUGH CENTRAL

America would shorten the water route between the East and West Coasts of the United States by thousands of miles. Instead of traveling all the way around the southern point of South America, ships would be able to bypass the continent entirely. It seemed to make sense to build the canal in Panama, an area of Central America then belonging to Colombia. There, the distance across the **isthmus** was shorter than anywhere else in Central America. However, building such a canal would not be a simple task.

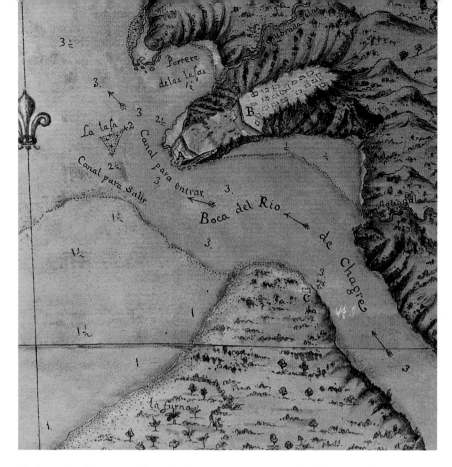

Before the Panama Canal was constructed, the Chagres River was known for powerful rapids that made travel by boat impossible.

Early Ideas

Successful completion of a canal would require the taming of the wild Chagres River, which led inland from the Caribbean Sea on the north coast of Panama. The river swelled during the rainy season. As a result, flooding and landslides were common. The land near the river's wild rapids made boat travel difficult. And the land was often covered in thick muck. The machinery needed to dig a canal could easily become coated in mud and quickly rust. In addition, canal builders would have to dig through miles of mountains to reach the Pacific Ocean on the southern coast of the country. They would also have to cope with deadly tropical diseases, especially malaria and yellow fever. Such obstacles made the task seem almost impossible.

In 1850, Dr. Edward Cullen of Great Britain's Royal Geographical Society made an announcement that gave new hope for the possibility of constructing a canal in Panama. Cullen claimed he had walked a trail from coast to coast that never rose more than 150 feet (46 meters) above sea level. It seemed too good to be true. The United States, France, England, and Colombia announced a joint **expedition** to Panama to investigate Cullen's claims.

Despite having been on previous expeditions in Central and South America, naval officer Isaac Strain failed in his exploration of Panama.

U.S. Navy lieutenant Isaac Strain arrived ahead of leaders from other nations. Eager to claim glory for his country, Strain and his men headed into the jungle. The men were carrying enough food for only a few days. They never found Cullen's trail and soon became hopelessly lost. Within a few weeks, their guns rusted. When a few of the men, including Strain, emerged on the Pacific coast, they were barely alive.

Crossing by Rail

The results of Strain's expedition shocked the nation. However, people were still determined to improve transportation across the isthmus. California's gold boom was under way, and people knew it would not reach its full potential without

YESTERDAY'S HEADLINES

In 1855, *Harper's* magazine published an article about Isaac Strain's ill-fated expedition across the Isthmus of Panama. As tales of the expedition began to spread, so did the idea that Panama was dangerous and mysterious. These beliefs were confirmed years later, when President Ulysses S. Grant (above) ordered several expeditions to map Panama and record every detail of its **climate** and landscape.

better transportation. A group of New York City merchants headed by William Henry Aspinwall had started the Pacific Mail Steamship Company in April 1848, even before they knew of gold in California. They planned to transport crops grown on California farms to the East Coast. Once the gold rush started, their ships transported gold and brought miners and **entrepreneurs** to the West Coast.

William Henry Aspinwall traveled on his Panama Railroad only a single time.

Aspinwall and his associates soon had the idea of building a railroad over the Isthmus of Panama. Workers encountered countless obstacles as they built the railroad. There were swamps 100 feet (30 m) deep, clouds of disease-carrying mosquitoes, stifling heat and humidity, and raging floods. The workers built bridges and saw them washed away a day later. Countless men died of cholera and yellow fever. Despite these setbacks, the Panama Railroad was completed in 1855. It took five years to finish and cost eight times the amount originally projected.

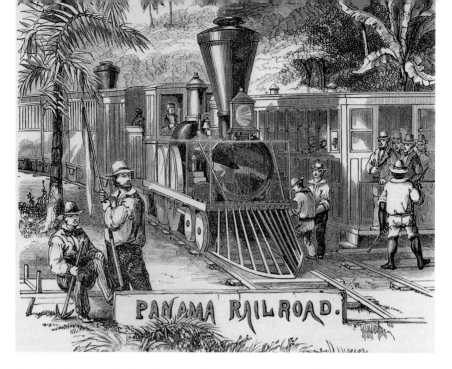

A train first made the journey from one coast of Panama to the other by the Panama Railroad on January 28, 1855.

The Panama Railroad was a major success, bringing huge amounts of money to its owners. This success brought worldwide attention to the area and led to more surveys of the isthmus. **Engineers** preparing surveys for the railroad had discovered a gap in the mountains at Culebra. Its elevation was just 275 feet (84 m) above sea level. This gap would eventually provide a path where the Panama Canal would be built.

Despite the railroad's success, Panama was not the only location considered for building a canal. Between 1870 and 1875, President Ulysses S. Grant ordered seven U.S. expeditions to different parts of Central America. Every location presented difficulties. Frequent floods made some places impractical for a canal. In addition, Central America's mountains all but ruled out a sea-level canal like Egypt's Suez Canal. In one part of Central America, the isthmus was less than 30 miles (48 kilometers) wide. However, the mountains were so high there that it would be necessary to build locks capable of raising ships more than 1,000 feet (305 m). Locks are sections of a canal with gates at each end. They are used for raising and lowering boats by changing the water level.

Another Canal

The Suez Canal had been built by French entrepreneur Ferdinand de Lesseps to link the Mediterranean and Red Seas in Egypt. The project was completed in an environment completely different from the one in Panama. There was no need to cut a passage through mountainous landscapes. There was also no prolonged rainy season, so there was no risk of the deadly landslides like the ones that threatened projects in Panama.

The Suez Canal stretches 101 miles (163 km) across Egypt, connecting the Mediterranean and Red Seas.

Ferdinand de Lesseps had correctly chosen a sea-level canal as the best solution. Yet even in conditions less challenging than those of Panama, the Suez Canal project took more than a decade to complete and cost more than twice its original estimate. Throughout the project, Lesseps worked tirelessly to secure private funding in France and Egypt. By the time the first ships steamed through Suez in November 1869, he was a hero in his homeland.

Onward to Panama

After his success with the Suez Canal, Lesseps was convinced that he could build another canal in Panama. However, he was unaware of how different the challenges of building a Central American canal would be.

The Suez Canal is an open-cut canal. This means it does not use locks to transition from its entrances to the seas on its ends.

Ferdinand de Lesseps (second row, middle), shown here with his team of engineers, was eventually sentenced to five years in prison for his mismanagement of the Panama Canal project.

Regardless, he expressed an interest in the project during the summer of 1875. Almost from the beginning, he resolved that the canal would be built without locks. He also favored following the path of the Panama Railroad.

U.S. engineers soon announced the results of their surveys. They determined that Panama was not the best location for a Central American canal. Instead, they favored a route across Nicaragua. Lesseps ignored these reports and continued to press for a canal in Panama. Soon after, a group of businessmen, the Türr Syndicate, took over the project, though Lesseps remained involved. The Türr Syndicate worked with the Colombian government to secure the rights to explore Panama.

ULYSSES S. GRANT'S LETTER TO NATHAN APPLETON

In 1881, former president Ulysses S. Grant wrote to Nathan Appleton, a U.S. government official in charge of working with France, to develop plans for a canal. In the letter, Grant expressed reservations about Ferdinand de Lesseps's plans for a sea-level canal in Panama. See page 60 for a link to read the letter online.

The French surveys were far less complete than President Grant's had been. All of the surveyors became extremely ill with malaria, and some died in the jungle. Those who survived struggled over steep landscapes in hot, humid weather. They sunk into the muck and grew exhausted battling the elements. Eventually, Colombia struck a new deal with the Türr Syndicate requiring a survey by an international team of engineers. Two years were given for organizing a canal company. Another 12 years were set aside for the construction of the canal. Ferdinand de Lesseps was convinced that the project would require no more than eight years. Eventually, construction began in 1881.

The Panama Canal Company

The Panama Canal Company struggled from the beginning. Lesseps knew that the Panama Railroad could play a crucial role in removing soil and excavated rock, especially at Culebra, where a gap in the mountains would provide an excellent route for the canal. As a result, the Panama Canal Company purchased the railway at a very high price. However, it never made much use of its purchase. Contractors were hired, only to withdraw soon afterward. Equipment arrived promptly, but too often it was not suited to the demands of the task. To make matters worse, workers were disorganized and unhappy in the harsh environment.

Panama's climate also raised several problems. Equipment rusted quickly and needed replacement often. Two years into the project, a huge earthquake rattled Panama and caused damage. When news of the earthquake reached Paris, **investors** were concerned

French engineers hired to work on the canal traveled to Panama with their families and servants.

because Lesseps had earlier claimed that Panama would not have any earthquakes. However, confidence in the Panama Canal Company was so high that investors continued to pour money into the project.

It was the environment itself that eventually defeated the project. **Excavation** was difficult and expensive, especially at Culebra. Downpours caused landslides on excavated slopes, filling the channel with rocks and mud. To prevent this, excavators had the idea of widening the channel and making its slopes less steep. This took more time and increased the cost of the project.

As support for the French Panama Canal project fell apart, construction equipment was abandoned and workers returned to their homes.

Worse, disease was widespread among the workers. Malaria and yellow fever, combined with accidents, claimed more than 22,000 lives. The causes of malaria and yellow fever were not yet understood, so health measures met with little success. After eight years, the project had barely begun. Ferdinand de Lesseps was 83 years old, and funding had dried up as investors lost faith in promises that were seldom fulfilled. By mid-May 1889, the constant hum of activity on the isthmus fell silent. The project had failed.

CHAPTER 2

CHANGING HANDS

When the French abandoned the Panama Canal project, there was still a great deal of work left to be completed.

By 1885, only one-sixth of the canal's excavation had been completed, and the cost to finish the project appeared likely to be double that of the original estimate. After the project failed, the truth about how the money was raised led to outrage.

Philippe-Jean Bunau-Varilla eventually became widely disliked by Panamanians for encouraging a treaty that gave the United States significant control over part of their country.

Money Trouble

The French government had allowed the Panama Canal Company to issue **bonds** to help pay for the canal. The company bribed bankers, members of the press, and several politicians to promote the bonds. Their efforts were unsuccessful. By January 1889, the company had gone bankrupt.

In all, some 800,000 people had invested in the Panama Canal Company. Many were ruined by these investments. By 1892, news of the bribes accepted by government ministers began to leak out. The bribed officials had hidden information about the failure of the Panama Canal Company. French citizens had continued pouring money into the doomed project, not knowing that their investments had little chance of succeeding. Several bribed officials, including Lesseps and his son Charles, were convicted of their crimes. However, their punishments were eventually suspended.

A new Panama Canal Company was formed to replace the failed organization. After the disaster of the earlier project, few dared to support the new company. The French government washed its hands of any association with the project. However, the group was eventually able to secure enough funding to continue the canal's construction. It extended its agreement with Colombia to continue digging, and excavation began in October 1894. The new company possessed very limited resources, so construction went slowly. As the project continued, the company began looking for a buyer.

The United States Steps In

The United States was still leaning toward building a canal across Nicaragua. Philippe-Jean Bunau-Varilla, an engineer with the Panama Canal Company, set about trying to convince U.S. officials to take over the Panama project instead. He pointed to the dangers of one of Nicaragua's volcanoes and claimed that Panama did not offer such risks. Through tireless efforts, he won them over. In 1902, the United States government purchased the holdings of the Panany Canal Company for $40 million. Plans for a canal in Nicaragua were scrapped.

Now the United States needed a long-term agreement from the Colombian government to complete the canal. U.S. secretary of state John Hay began negotiating terms with Tomás Herrán, a Colombian official serving in the United States. The two reached an agreement in January 1903. The United States would take control of the land surrounding the canal route. In return, it would pay $10 million to the Colombian government, followed by yearly payments of $250,000. The U.S. government approved this plan, but the Colombian government did not.

John Hay served as U.S. secretary of state from 1898 to 1905.

Rebellion in Colombia

Not all Colombians were opposed to a U.S. canal in Panama. Several politicians in Panama saw the canal project as an opportunity to seek independence from Colombia. Dr. Manuel Amador Guerrero traveled to the United States in 1903 to seek support for a rebellion in Panama. He also gathered support from Panama's military commanders. The **separatist** rebellion was set to take place in November.

A VIEW FROM ABROAD

Though Colombian foreign minister Tomás Herrán reached an agreement with the U.S. government concerning the use of land in Panama, the Colombian government rejected the terms. This was partly because the country hoped to secure a larger payment from the United States. However, the agreement was also rejected because Herrán had negotiated without his country's approval. Lawmakers in Colombia did not consider Herrán's efforts to be an official representation of the country.

At the last moment, it seemed that the carefully designed plan would unravel. Tomás Arias, an influential rebel leader, decided to back out at the last minute. Within hours, Colombian sharpshooters were on their way to the port city of Colón, Panama. However, they knew nothing of the revolution brewing there. Instead, they were responding to a rumor that Nicaragua was

YESTERDAY'S HEADLINES

President Theodore Roosevelt's decision to send U.S. ships to Panama during and after the separatist revolution raised objections both at home and abroad. The *New York Times* published an article criticizing Roosevelt's "act of sordid conquest." Elsewhere, political cartoonist Charles Green Bush depicted Roosevelt as an armed soldier pointing a huge cannon at helpless Colombia. Despite such criticism, Roosevelt believed he had made the right choice and defended his decision throughout his presidency.

plotting to invade northern Panama.

At 5:30 p.m. on November 2, the gunboat USS *Nashville* dropped anchor in the nearby harbor. At midnight, the Colombian ship *Cartagena* arrived with 500 armed troops. A tense situation seemed ready to explode. However, it never did.

Within a week, several more U.S. gunboats arrived near Colón. They blocked Colombian troops from landing and going ashore to put down the revolution. U.S. troops also made their way onto land, ruining any plans the Colombians might have made to march overland through the jungle to reach Panama. Thanks to this intervention by the United States, Panamanian leaders were able to declare independence from Colombia without combat.

After the separatist revolution, U.S. troops were stationed in Panama to protect the Panama Railroad and the canal's construction site.

The United States quickly granted official recognition to the new nation of Panama. Several other nations followed. With its Panamanian allies now in charge of the land surrounding the canal route, the United States was finally free to proceed with the canal project.

A FIRSTHAND LOOK AT
ROOSEVELT'S JANUARY 4, 1904, MESSAGE TO CONGRESS

President Theodore Roosevelt was criticized for his role in the Panamanian revolution. On January 4, 1904, he wrote a message to Congress that defended his action and declared the construction of the Panama Canal to be a "great work for civilization." See page 60 for a link to read the message online.

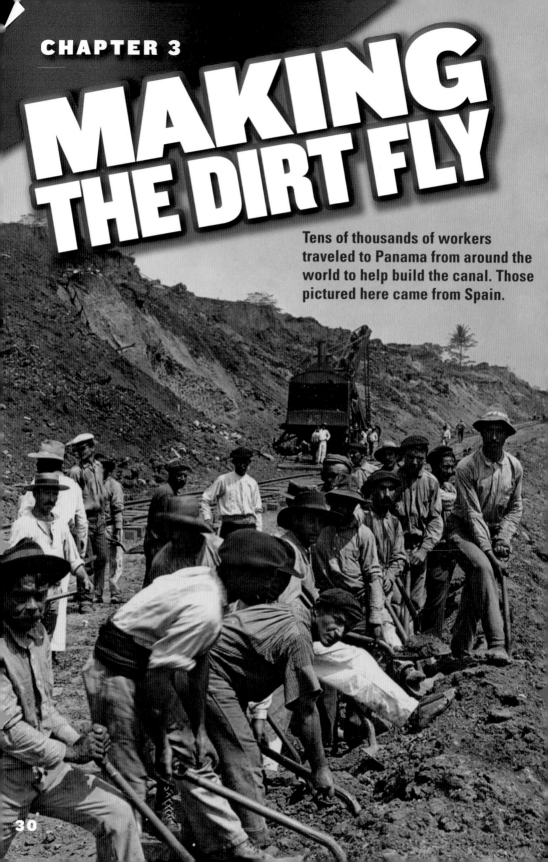

CHAPTER 3

MAKING THE DIRT FLY

Tens of thousands of workers traveled to Panama from around the world to help build the canal. Those pictured here came from Spain.

WITH THE WAY CLEARED BY Panama's revolution, the United States finalized its purchase of the Panama Canal Company's holdings. Of the $40 million it paid the company, roughly $30 million of it was for the excavations that had already been completed. The other $10 million was for machines, buildings, and the Panama Railroad. In addition, the United States paid the newly independent nation of Panama $10 million for the right to control the Canal Zone, a strip of land 10 miles (16 km) wide along the canal route.

John Findlay Wallace was given a salary of $25,000 per year for serving as chief engineer of the Panama Canal, making him more highly paid than any U.S. government employee except for the president.

Lessons Learned

Though the United States would have liked to have begun excavating Culebra and building locks immediately, the difficulties faced by the original Panama Canal Company provided an important lesson. U.S. leaders decided to prepare very carefully before going forward with construction of the canal. President Theodore Roosevelt established a commission of seven men, called the Isthmian Canal Commission (ICC), to guide the project. John Findlay Wallace was appointed chief engineer.

Though Wallace had plenty of experience with large building projects, he was overwhelmed almost from the beginning. Before work on the canal could begin, it would be necessary to repair and replace much of the machinery that had been purchased from the French. New buildings were needed to house workers and supplies. In addition, the Panama Railroad would require a great deal of rebuilding. Perhaps most importantly, the problems of malaria and yellow fever would have to be solved.

William Gorgas, a doctor and U.S. Army colonel, was appointed to

TODAY'S PERSPECTIVE

When William Gorgas arrived in Panama to help prevent the spread of malaria and yellow fever, he knew his task would be difficult. These diseases are spread by mosquitoes, which use water as their breeding grounds. But by aggressively searching for and killing the mosquitoes, Gorgas managed to rid the Canal Zone of diseases carried by mosquitoes. At the time, many people in the Canal Zone were skeptical of his work, but it proved effective and became a standard approach for dealing with such diseases. If not for his groundbreaking work, the building of the Panama Canal may not have been possible.

deal with these deadly diseases. In the years since the French canal project was ruined by tropical sicknesses, the causes of both malaria and yellow fever had been discovered. British doctor Ronald Ross had discovered that malaria is transmitted by the *Anopheles* mosquito. Cuban doctor Carlos Finlay had concluded that yellow fever was caused by another mosquito species, *Aedes aegypti*. Both types of mosquitoes were common in Panama. Finally, the outbreaks that had crippled the French project made sense. Gorgas soon developed a plan for eliminating yellow fever and malaria in Panama by removing mosquitoes from the work area.

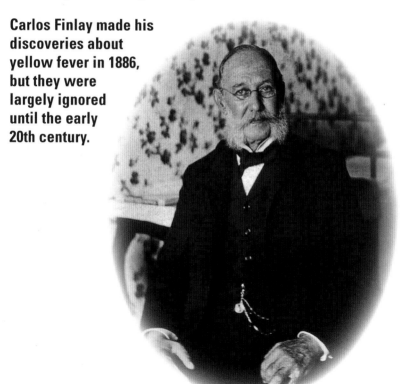

Carlos Finlay made his discoveries about yellow fever in 1886, but they were largely ignored until the early 20th century.

After helping make the Canal Zone safe for workers by eliminating disease-spreading mosquitoes, William C. Gorgas became surgeon general of the U.S. Army in 1914.

Further Preparations

For nearly two years, U.S. engineers busied themselves mostly with improving the **infrastructure** needed to complete the project. They used what they could of the buildings and equipment the French had left, and replaced the rest. Meanwhile, Gorgas tackled the challenge of ridding the Canal Zone of mosquitoes. However, his methods were met with resistance from chief engineer Wallace. Frustrated by the overwhelming complexity of the project, Wallace resigned in June 1905. His choice to leave the project was made easier by the epidemic of yellow fever that raged in Panama at the time. During this "Great Scare," the disease

John Frank Stevens was appointed chief engineer based on his work expanding railroads into the western United States.

claimed so many victims that coffins were stacked on the railway platform at Colón. Most U.S. workers feared they would become infected and fled the area.

John Frank Stevens replaced Wallace on July 26. At the same time, Roosevelt simplified the ICC by placing it in the hands of a committee of just three members. With Stevens's full support, Gorgas was finally free to put his plan into action without restriction. He divided Panama into 25 districts and appointed inspectors for each one. The inspectors searched buildings and looked for mosquito nests to destroy. Swamps in the Canal Zone were drained to prevent mosquitoes from breeding there. People confirmed to be infected with yellow fever or malaria were **quarantined**. By the following year, yellow fever had been eliminated completely and malaria deaths had been reduced dramatically.

Help Wanted

The efforts of Gorgas and his inspectors helped make Panama more attractive to American workers. To continue to draw new employees, the ICC built clubhouses, ice cream parlors, and libraries in the Canal Zone. It also constructed baseball fields and set up baseball leagues for the canal workers.

The Panama Canal Company provided workers with small, simple homes to live in.

A FIRSTHAND LOOK AT
PRESIDENT ROOSEVELT'S VISIT TO PANAMA

When President Roosevelt visited Panama in 1906, he became the first U.S. president ever to leave the country while in office. He climbed aboard a massive steam shovel to create one of the most memorable images of the Panama Canal era. See page 60 for a link to view the photo online.

President Roosevelt had appointed newspaperman Joseph Bucklin Bishop, a close friend of his, executive secretary of the ICC in 1905. Bishop worked tirelessly to raise workers' spirits in the Canal Zone. He founded a weekly newspaper called the *Canal Record* for the workers in Panama. The paper reported on the canal's

Some worker housing, such as the buildings pictured in the foreground, was left over from the original French attempt to build the canal.

George Washington Goethals (left) was a colonel in the
U.S. Army Corps of Engineers. He had previously overseen
construction of the Riverton Lock in Alabama.

progress, allowing the men to see that their efforts were
helping to complete the project. The *Canal Record* also
included write-ups of the workers' baseball games and
underlined the positive benefits of life on the isthmus.
The news filtered its way into newspapers back in the
United States. Americans were fascinated by the progress
of the canal. They encouraged their representatives in
Congress to keep the project steaming ahead.

The Building Begins

Roosevelt decided to place the excavation and
construction of the canal in the hands of the U.S. Army
Corps of Engineers. He appointed George Washington

Workers used explosives to blast through rock during the construction of the canal.

Goethals to direct the project under the supervision of chief engineer Stevens. When Stevens resigned, Goethals was chosen to replace him. Goethals immediately split the project into three divisions—Atlantic, Central, and Pacific—and appointed a director for each one.

Major William Sibert led the Atlantic Division, which was in charge of building the entrance to the canal at Colón, as well as the Gatun Locks and the Gatun Dam across the Chagres River. Engineer Sydney Williamson directed the construction of the Pacific entrance, in addition to the Pedro Miguel and Miraflores Locks and the dams needed for their operation. The Central Division, led by David DuBose Gaillard, was entrusted with a project almost impossible to imagine. It needed to lower the mountains to a height of 40 feet (12 m) over a distance of 8 miles (13 km) at Culebra!

Mighty Machinery

The immense scale of the canal project called for advanced technology to meet its demands. More than 100 huge, railroad-mounted steam shovels scooped up excavated dirt and rock and dumped it onto flat railcars. Loose soil was hauled to other sites, like Gatun Dam, and

Steam-powered railcars allowed workers to move rubble and dirt out of the way as they blasted through mountains and other obstacles.

GATUN LOCKS
PANAMA CANAL
1913

The Panama Canal Locks

The Panama Canal's lock system lifts ships entering from either the Atlantic or Pacific Ocean up to the elevation of Gatun Lake and the rest of the canal. The lifting at each end is done in three stages. When a ship reaches the locks, electric locomotives guide it into the massive concrete lock chamber. Each one is 110 feet (34 m) wide and 1,050 feet (320 m) long. This sets a maximum limit on the size of the ships that can pass through the canal. In the lock, lake water moves rapidly through huge tunnels that empty into the bottom of the chamber. As the chamber fills, the ship rises. Going from the bottom to the top of the locks takes only eight minutes, but requires 26.7 million gallons (101 million liters) of water! To lower a ship from the canal to ocean level, the chamber is slowly drained.

used to fill holes or level off hilly ground. Large sections of the rebuilt Panama Railroad were lifted with steam-powered cranes and moved to new excavation sites. This saved time and manpower, and made it possible to progress at a much faster rate.

Air-powered drills were used to make holes for explosives. Compressed air to operate the drills was piped in from three plants 5 miles (8 km) from the Culebra work site. A single blast might use as much as 200 pounds (91 kilograms) of dynamite, set in holes drilled 27 feet (8 m) deep! By 1907, 100 steam shovels, 560 drills, and 50 steam cranes worked daily in the Canal

Zone. Every year, the project required 500,000 barrels of oil and more than 700 million pounds (318 million kg) of coal. In all, 30 million pounds (14 million kg) of dynamite were used.

Building the Locks

The construction of the canal's colossal locks began in 1909. A relay system of cranes, railcars, steam locomotives, and cableways lifted full buckets of concrete and returned empty ones. Near the lock floor, the locks' sidewalls were 50 feet (15 m) thick. Some of the steel lock gates were 82 feet (25 m) high. The pipes carrying water to the locks were 15 feet (5 m) in diameter.

Workers perched high above the ground on scaffolding as they worked on the massive gates of the canal's locks.

CHAPTER 4

A LIVING THING

Hugh crowds of workers saw the rewards of their efforts as the tugboat *Gatun* traveled through the Gatun Locks for the first time.

THE LOCKS WERE FINISHED by June 1913. Gatun Dam's **spillway** gates were closed and Gatun Lake began to rise. By September of that year, excavation at Culebra was completed. To test the Gatun Locks, a tugboat named *Gatun* was lifted step by step to Gatun Lake as thousands of spectators looked on with awe and pride. The same week, Culebra Cut, now renamed Gaillard Cut, was filled in spectacular fashion. President Woodrow Wilson pressed a button in Washington, D.C., that sent a telegraph signal to Panama, initiating the detonation of hundreds of dynamite charges. Water poured into the cut, connecting it with Gatun Lake.

The SS *Ancon* traveled through the canal during its official opening ceremony on August 15, 1914.

Open for Business

On January 7, 1914, the French crane boat *Alexandre La Valley* made the first full trip through the Panama Canal. On August 3, 1914, the cement boat *Cristobal* became the first oceangoing ship to make the trip. Hardly anyone noticed the event, however, because World War I (1914–1918) broke out in Europe the same day. The Panama Canal suddenly seemed like old news.

The canal was largely ignored during the war. On average, only five ships per day crossed the isthmus. The canal's traffic began to increase when the war ended. In July 1919, 33 U.S. ships returning from war in Europe crossed the canal in a little more than two days. Within a few years, traffic across the isthmus had tripled. The strategic importance of the Panama Canal continued to grow, and it would greatly benefit the U.S. Navy during World War II (1939–1945).

At the same time, ships were getting larger. BB-45 Colorado class battleships, which first appeared in 1917, were 97.5 feet (29.7 m) wide. They safely fit into the canal locks. BB-49 South Dakota class battleships appeared three years later. They were 106 feet (32.3 m) wide and barely squeezed into the locks at Panama. By 1934, some battleships stretched a foot wider. If the U.S.

Ships such as the USS *Colorado* were small enough to travel through the Panama Canal without difficulty.

military built its ships any wider, they would not fit into the locks. As a result, the United States began building a third, larger set of locks in 1939 to accommodate newer warships. However, the project was suspended when the United States entered World War II in 1941. Because the country's European allies offered naval resources, it wasn't as necessary to transport larger U.S. ships from the Pacific to the Atlantic.

The battleship USS *Arizona* was completely destroyed when the Japanese military attacked the Pearl Harbor U.S. Naval Base on December 7, 1941, pulling the United States into World War II.

Political Problems

The Panama Canal came to be a major source of argument between the United States and Panama. Many Panamanians believed that the United States should hand over control of the canal to the government of Panama. By the end of World War II, these Panamanian nationalists had grown frustrated with the United States. Not long after December 1946, when the United States proposed extending its control over the Canal Zone another 20 years, nationalists armed with guns and machetes forced the Panamanian

YESTERDAY'S HEADLINES

Despite the careful planning of the ICC and the hard work of its employees, the Panama Canal has struggled continuously against resistance from nature. In October 1914, a wall collapsed at the Gaillard Cut, forcing the canal to be closed. In September 1915, at the height of the rainy season in Panama, an avalanche of rock and mud closed the cut for seven months.

In order to prevent mudslides and avalanches from filling in the canal completely, the waterway must be dredged often. Dredging is a form of excavating that is done underwater. Workers use machines to pull mud from the bottom of the canal and move it elsewhere.

A VIEW FROM ABR★AD

The 1989 U.S. invasion of Panama was widely approved within the United States. But many other nations spoke out against the action. They believed it to be an unnecessary act of aggression. However, many Panamanians favored the overthrow of military governor Manuel Noriega, who was a harsh and corrupt leader. Despite the controversy over the invasion, it accomplished the goal of keeping the Panama Canal a neutral zone that could be freely used by many nations.

government to reject the offer. Within a year, the U.S. military had removed its forces from all its Panamanian bases outside the Canal Zone to protect the military from attacks. A decade later, U.S. troops clashed with student demonstrators in the Canal Zone. Tensions continued to build when the United States agreed to fly the Panamanian flag at only one location in the Canal Zone.

In 1964, the Panamanian nationalists' frustrations came to a boil. Around 200 students, carrying the Panamanian flag, marched on the Canal Zone on January 9. The flag was torn in the struggle that followed. Violence erupted in response. More than 20 people were killed and hundreds more were injured. Relations between the two countries gradually improved, but the tensions that gave rise to the 1964 revolt were never far beneath the surface.

In 1977, U.S. president Jimmy Carter signed two treaties with Panamanian general Omar Torrijos, who had seized power nearly a decade before and was popular among most Panamanians. The Torrijos-Carter Treaties provided for transfer of the canal to Panama on December 31, 1999. The U.S. Senate eventually approved both treaties. However, some U.S. politicians expressed concern over giving up control of such an important strategic asset.

By 1989, the treaties were endangered. Four U.S. military officers were held up at a roadblock on December 16. They were quickly surrounded by an angry mob of Panamanians. When members of the mob opened fire, one of the U.S. officials was killed. The United States responded by invading Panama. Manuel Noriega, the military governor of Panama, was captured and removed from power. The country rebuilt its government, and on December 31, 1999, it took ownership of the Panama Canal Zone.

A FIRSTHAND LOOK AT
RESISTANCE TO THE TORRIJOS-CARTER TREATIES

In 1999, with the transfer of the Canal Zone to Panama quickly approaching, members of Congress tried unsuccessfully to have the Torrijos-Carter Treaties declared void. See page 60 for a link to read their proposed bill online.

MAP OF THE EVENTS

What Happened Where?

ATLANTIC OCEAN
(Caribbean Sea)

Colón ●

...ón

...903, U.S. gunboats patrolled the
...ters near Colón to prevent Colombian
...ps from going ashore to put down the
...olution in Panama.

Third set of loc...
(under construc...

Gatun Locks ▯ ▯

...un Locks

...s set of locks raises ships up into the
...ama Canal from the Atlantic Ocean.

Gatun Lake

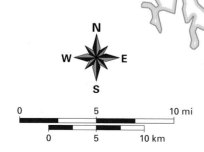

```
        N
   W ✦ E
        S
```

```
0          5          10 mi
|————————|————————|
0          5          10 km
```

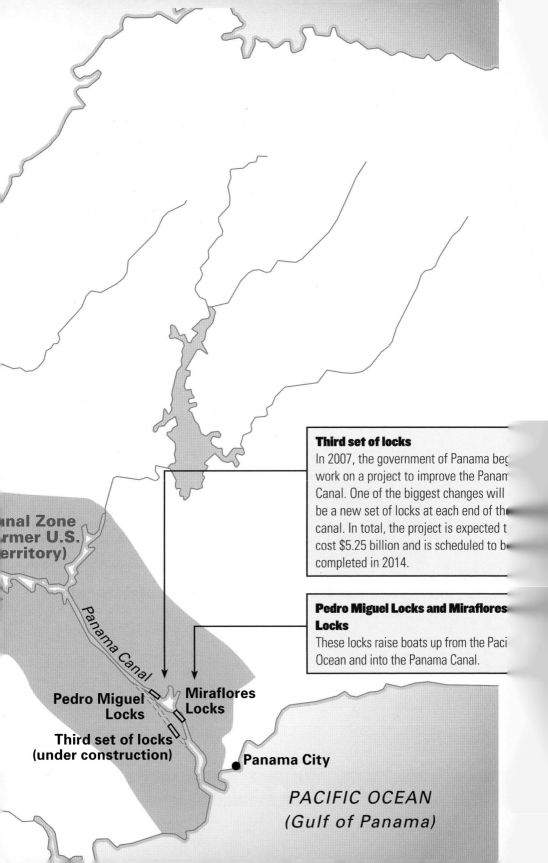

Third set of locks

In 2007, the government of Panama beg[an] work on a project to improve the Panam[a] Canal. One of the biggest changes will be a new set of locks at each end of th[e] canal. In total, the project is expected t[o] cost $5.25 billion and is scheduled to b[e] completed in 2014.

Pedro Miguel Locks and Miraflores Locks

These locks raise boats up from the Paci[fic] Ocean and into the Panama Canal.

Canal Zone
[fo]rmer U.S.
[te]rritory)

Panama Canal

Pedro Miguel
Locks

Miraflores
Locks

Third set of locks
(under construction)

● **Panama City**

PACIFIC OCEAN
(Gulf of Panama)

Going Through Changes

Today, even massive cruise ships can pass through the Panama Canal safely.

Today, 12,000 to 15,000 ships pass through the Panama Canal each year. Many of those ships are much larger than the ones used when the canal was being built more than 100 years ago. In 2006, Panamanian citizens approved a measure to expand the Panama Canal by building a third set of locks able to handle larger ships. Dredging ensures that the canal is deep enough for these ships.

The changes have sped up the growth of cities along the canal as new jobs are created. But this growth has had a harmful impact on the environment. As trees along the canal are cut down to make room for buildings, there is less water to fill the canal in dry seasons. To make matters worse, laws do not protect the forest along the canal. If such expansion continues, there might not be enough water to operate the locks. The Panama Canal would have to suspend operation for months at a time. It will take careful planning and responsible use of resources to ensure that the canal stays open for many years to come.

Though dredging helps keep the Panama Canal deep, around 10 percent of the world's ships cannot currently fit through it.

40 MILES (64 KM) LONG.

Ferdinand de Lesseps

John Frank Stevens

Ferdinand de Lesseps (1805–1894) was a French diplomat who organized the successful Suez Canal project and the disastrous French attempt to build a canal in Panama.

Isaac Strain (1821–1857) was a U.S. Navy lieutenant who led an ill-fated expedition into Panama's wilderness.

John Findlay Wallace (1852–1921) was the first chief engineer of the Isthmian Canal Commission. Though he had a great deal of experience with large building projects, he was overwhelmed by the canal.

John Frank Stevens (1853–1943) replaced John Findlay Wallace as chief engineer of the Isthmian Canal Commission. He supported William Gorgas's work to end disease in the Canal Zone, and other measures to build the infrastructure for a successful operation.

William Gorgas (1854–1920) was a U.S. Army surgeon who planned and carried out the removal of mosquitoes in Panama to prevent the spread of yellow fever and malaria among canal workers.

Theodore Roosevelt (1858–1919) was the 26th president of the United States. He was the driving force behind the U.S. construction of the Panama Canal.

William Gorgas

George Washington Goethals (1858–1928) was chief engineer for the Panama Canal project after John Frank Stevens. He was a genius of management as well as engineering.

Philippe-Jean Bunau-Varilla (1859–1940) tirelessly lobbied the U.S. government to build a canal in Panama instead of Nicaragua.

TIMELINE

1850
Dr. Edward Cullen claims to have found a trail across Panama, giving people hope that a canal can be built there.

1850–1855
The Panama Railroad is constructed.

1881
The French Panama Canal Company begins construction of the Panama Canal.

1904
U.S. construction begins on the canal.

1906
President Roosevelt visits the Canal Zone.

1909
Work begins on the Panama Canal locks.

1964
Panamanian nationalists riot in the Canal Zone.

1977
The Torrijos-Carter Treaties promise that the United States will hand over control of the canal to Panama in 1999.

1889

The French Panama Canal Company goes bankrupt.

1902

The U.S. government purchases the Panama Canal Company.

1903

The Panamanian revolution frees Panama from Colombian rule.

1913

The canal's locks are completed.

1914

The Panama Canal officially opens.

1948

The U.S. military evacuates its Panamanian bases that are outside the Canal Zone.

1989

The United States invades Panama and overthrows military governor Manuel Noriega.

1999

The Panama Canal is turned over to Panamanian control.

2006

Panamanians approve an expansion project to add a new set of locks to the canal.

LIVING HISTORY

Primary sources provide firsthand evidence about a topic. Witnesses to a historical event create primary sources. They include autobiographies, newspaper reports of the time, oral histories, photographs, and memoirs. A secondary source analyzes primary sources and is one step or more removed from the event. Secondary sources include textbooks, encyclopedias, and commentaries. To view the following primary and secondary sources, go to www.factsfornow.scholastic.com. Enter the keywords **Panama Canal** and look for the Living History logo Σ¦.

Σ¦ **President Roosevelt's Visit to Panama** President Theodore Roosevelt visited the Panama Canal Zone in 1906. While in Panama, Roosevelt posed aboard a steam shovel for one of the most memorable photos of the canal's construction.

Σ¦ **Resistance to the Torrijos-Carter Treaties** In 1999, the United States prepared to hand over control of the Panama Canal to Panama as agreed in the Torrijos-Carter Treaties of 1977. Some members of the U.S. Congress argued that it would be foolish to hand over control of such an important location. Their attempted bill striking down the treaties was unsuccessful.

Σ¦ **Roosevelt's January 4, 1904, Message to Congress** President Theodore Roosevelt was criticized for helping to encourage the revolution that led to Panama's separation from Colombia. On January 4, 1904, he wrote a message to Congress in which he defended his actions.

Σ¦ **Ulysses S. Grant's Letter to Nathan Appleton** Ferdinand de Lesseps designed a plan for a canal in Panama that did not use locks. However, U.S. engineers determined that it would be impossible to build such a canal in Panama. In 1881, Ulysses S. Grant wrote a letter disapproving Lesseps's plans.

RESOURCES

Books

DuTemple, Lesley A. *The Panama Canal*. Minneapolis: Lerner, 2003.

Garraty, John. *Theodore Roosevelt: American Rough Rider*. New York: Sterling Publishing Company, 2007.

Hall, M. C. *Panama Canal*. Vero Beach, FL: Rourke Publishing, 2010.

Roberts, Russell. *Building the Panama Canal*. Hockessin, DE: Mitchell Lane Publishers, 2009.

Shields, Charles J. *Panama*. Broomall, PA: Mason Crest Publishers, 2009.

Visit this Scholastic Web site for more information on the Panama Canal:
www.factsfornow.scholastic.com
Enter the keywords Panama Canal

GLOSSARY

bonds (BAHNDS) documents that allow companies or governments to raise money; people buy the bonds and are later paid back, with interest added

climate (KLYE-mit) the weather typical of a place over a long period of time

engineers (en-juh-NEERZ) people trained to design and build machines or large structures such as bridges and roads

entrepreneurs (ahn-truh-pruh-NURZ) people who start businesses or find new ways to make money

excavation (ek-skuh-VAY-shun) the digging of a large hole in the ground to prepare for a construction project

expedition (ek-spuh-DISH-uhn) a long trip made for a specific purpose, such as exploration

infrastructure (IN-fruh-struk-chur) the underlying foundation of something or the system of public works such as roads and railroads

investors (in-VES-turz) people who give or lend money with the intention of getting more money back later

isthmus (IS-muhs) a narrow strip of land connecting two larger landmasses

quarantined (KWOR-uhn-teened) kept away from others for a period of time to stop a disease from spreading

separatist (SEP-ruh-tist) someone who holds the belief that his or her region should be independent from the control of another government

spillway (SPIL-way) a passage for extra water to flow over or around a dam

INDEX

Page numbers in *italics* indicate illustrations.

ABOUT THE AUTHOR

Peter Benoit earned a degree in mathematics at Skidmore College. He is an educator and poet. He has written more than four dozen books for Scholastic/Children's Press on topics including disasters, Native Americans, ecosystems, the *Titanic*, the electoral college, and the 2012 election. He has also written several books on crucial moments in American history and books on ancient Greece and ancient Rome. Benoit resides in Greenwich, New York.